From Power Plant to House

Colleen Hord

rourkeeducationalmedia.com

*Scan for Related Titles
and Teacher Resources*

Teaching Focus:
Concepts of Print- Have students find capital letters and punctuation in a sentence. Ask students to explain the purpose for using them in a sentence.

Before Reading:

Building Academic Vocabulary and Background Knowledge
Before reading a book, it is important to set the stage for your child or students by using pre-reading strategies. This will help them develop their vocabulary, increase their reading comprehension, and make connections across the curriculum.

1. *Read the title and look at the cover. Let's make predictions about what this book will be about.*
2. *Take a picture walk by talking about the pictures/photographs in the book. Implant the vocabulary as you take the picture walk. Be sure to talk about the text features such as headings, Table of Contents, glossary, bolded words, captions, charts/ diagrams, or Index.*
3. Have students read the first page of text with you then have students read the remaining text.
4. *Strategy Talk – use to assist students while reading.*
   - *Get your mouth ready*
   - *Look at the picture*
   - *Think…does it make sense*
   - *Think…does it look right*
   - *Think…does it sound right*
   - *Chunk it – by looking for a part you know*
5. *Read it again.*
6. *After reading the book complete the activities below.*

Content Area Vocabulary
Use glossary words in a sentence.

appliances
bill
devices
generators
power plant
transformer

After Reading:

Comprehension and Extension Activity
After reading the book, work on the following questions with your child or students in order to check their level of reading comprehension and content mastery.

1. *Why are electrical wires connected high above the ground?* (Inferring)
2. *Where does electricity come from?* (Summarize)
3. *Can you name three things that you use that need electricity?* (Text to self connection)
4. *What happens if people use more electricity than what is being made at the power plant?* (Inferring)

Extension Activity
Saving energy! What are some ways you can save energy at home or school? Take a walk around your classroom or house and write down things you see that use energy. How can we save some of the energy? Present your ideas by making a poster to display at home or at school showing ways everyone can save electricity.

The electricity you have in your home is like having an invisible super power living with you.

Flip a switch and you have light!

Push the microwave button and your food is cooked!

Electricity is what powers up the **appliances** and **devices** you use in your home each day.

Electricity starts its way to your house from the **power plant**.

Many people work at the power plant.

Some power plant workers take care of machines called **generators**. The generators help make the electricity.

Job Shop

If you are curious about how things work, working with generators might be a job for you.

Other workers keep track of how much electricity is being made from the generators. They make sure there is enough electricity for everyone.

Job Shop

Power plant workers use computers to monitor how much electricity is being made and how much is being used.

From the power plant, the electricity travels through wires to a large **transformer**.

Workers called linemen take wires from the transformer and attach them to poles high above the ground.

Job Shop

Linemen climb high poles to check wires. After storms, they may work long hours repairing wires until everyone has electricity again.

Wires from the poles go to a meter box attached to your house. Workers called meter readers check the numbers on the meter to see how much electricity your family is using.

The office worker at the electric company mails your family a **bill**. The bill tells how much money you have to pay for the electricity you used.

Job Shop

Besides having good math and computer skills, the office workers have to be good with answering customer's questions.

The invisible power of electricity reaches your house with the help of many hard workers.

Photo Glossary

 **appliances** (uh-PLYE-uhnss-iz): Machines made to do a certain job in the kitchen.

 **bill** (bil): A piece of paper that tells you how much money you must pay for something.

 **devices** (di-VISSE-iz): Pieces of equipment that do a special job.

 **generators** (JEN-uh-ray-turz): Machines that make electricity by turning a magnet inside a wire.

 **power plant** (POUR-ur plant): A building where electricity is made.

 **transformer** (trans-FOR-mer): A piece of equipment that changes the amount of electricity that goes into an electrical wire.

Index

Websites to Visit

www.enwin.com/kids/electricity/energy_electricity.cfm

www.tvakids.com

www.alliantenergykids.com/PlayingItSafe/ElectricSafety/000552

About the Author

Colleen Hord is an elementary teacher. She lives on six acres with her husband, chickens, ducks and peacocks. Writer's Workshop is her favorite part of her teaching day. When she isn't teaching or writing, she enjoys kayaking, walking on the beach, and gardening.

Meet The Author!
www.meetREMauthors.com

© 2015 Rourke Educational Media

www.rourkeeducationalmedia.com

PHOTO CREDITS: Cover © michaeljung, Dmytro Vietrov; Title Page © Elzbieta Sekowska; Page 3 © Steve Cole/christie & cole studio inc.; Page 4 © Ivan Pesic; Page 5 © jane; Page 6, 7 © Andrey_Popov; Page 8 © Aaron Kohr; Page 9 © Jackf; Page 11 © Tina Jeans; Page 13 © ndoeljindoel; Page 14 © HONGQI ZHANG; Page 15 © michaeljung; Page 17 © Nicole S. Young; Page 19 © fstop123; Page 20 © pablocalvog; Page 21 © kali9

Edited by: Luana Mitten
Cover and Interior design by: Jen Thomas

Library of Congress PCN Data

From Power Plant to House/ Colleen Hord
(Little World Communities and Commerce)
ISBN (hard cover)(alk. paper) 978-1-63430-061-2
ISBN (soft cover) 978-1-63430-091-9
ISBN (e-Book) 978-1-63430-118-3
Library of Congress Control Number: 2014953341
Printed in the United States of America, North Mankato, Minnesota

Also Available as:

ROURKE'S e-Books